funeral of the minstrel

I0171403

SPM
Publications

London

SPM Publications
Unit 136, 113-115 George Lane, South Woodford,
London E18 1AB, United Kingdom

www.spmpublications.com
www.sentinelwriting.com

First published in Great Britain by SPM Publications –
an imprint of Sentinel Writing & Publishing Company
Limited in October 2015.

ISBN 978-0-9927055-7-2

Front Cover by Olu Oguibe
Cover image: Olu Oguibe 'Untitled' 2010
Set in Palatino Linotype

Nnorom Azuonye

Poet, Playwright, Publisher and Preacher Nnorom Azuonye studied Dramatic Arts at the University of Nigeria, Nsukka, where he distinguished himself professionally and academically, winning the departmental Best Graduating Student Prize for 1989/90 session.

A versatile theatre artist, he has directed *Maama* by Kwesi Kay and designed the set for Ebrahim Hussein's *Kinjeketile*. His numerous stage roles include Sergeant in Femi Osofisan's *Once Upon Four Robbers*, Forest Head in Wole Soyinka's *A Dance of the Forests*, Dr Innocent Egbunike in Nnamdi Ndu's *Scars the Mar* and Chief Isokipiri Erekosima in Esiaba Irobi's *Hangmen Also Die*.

In 1990 Nnorom's play; *A Tasty Taboo* was performed at the University of Nigeria Arts Theatre and in 1994, his short play; *Return of the Businessman* was translated into Igbo language and broadcast on DITV Kaduna. In 2003 he co-wrote the screenplay for *Echoes of War* – an Obi Emelonye film.

Author of *Letter to God & Other Poems* (2003), *The Bridge Selection: Poems for the Road* (2005, 2012) and *We Need God in Nigeria Again* (2014), Nnorom's poems, short stories, essays and interviews have appeared in several international magazines, journals and anthologies including *Weekly Star*,

Agenda, Orbis, World Haiku Review, Theatre Forum,
Flair, Opon Ifa, Drumvoices Revue, Sketchbook,
Poetry Monthly, Eclectica Magazine, For the Love of
God, Sentinel Annual Literature Anthology, and
Poems for a Liminal Age.

Nnorom lives in London with his wife Thelma
Amaka (nee Mbomi), sons Arinze Chinedum and
Obinna Chiemelie, and daughter Nwachi Ola.

He blogs at: theblogazette.nnoromazuonye.com

Nnorom Azuonye

w. www.nnoromazuonye.com
f. https://www.facebook.com/nnorom.azuonye
t. https://twitter.com/nnoromazuonye

FUNERAL OF THE MINSTREL
A play

NNOROM AZUONYE

SPM Publications

Also by Nnorom Azuonye

Fiction

The Magenta Shadow (A collection of short stories)
Forthcoming 2016

Drama

A Tasty Taboo (a play) Forthcoming 2016.

Poetry

We Need God in Nigeria Again (2014)
The Bridge Selection: Poems for the Road (2005, 2012)
Letter to God & Other Poems (2003)

Anthologies

The Genesis of Falcon (Editor) 2013
Sentinel Annual Literature Anthology (Co-editor.)
2011.
Blue Hyacinths (Co-editor.) 2010

To the memory of Esiaba Irobi (1960 – 2010),
my teacher, mentor and friend.

Acknowledgments

Many thanks to Olu Oguibe for a powerful front cover and the untitled image of the casket draped with the Biafran flag.

A version of *Funeral of the Minstrel* was published in *Sentinel Annual Literature Anthology* 2011.

The poems 'Sisyphus' and 'Homecoming' quoted in this play are taken from *Why I Don't Like Philip Larkin & Other Poems* by Esiaba Irobi (Nsibidi Africana Publishers), 'Kingdom of the Mad' is taken from *Sentinel Poetry (online)* Issue #8, July 2003.

Contents

Preface: Esiaba Irobi, the Intellectual Terrorist   11

Funeral of the Minstrel   25

Important Notice

The characters in this play are fictitious except for Earthquake (Silas Ugwoke) and Esiaba Irobi who were real persons. However, the roles played by Earthquake and Esiaba Irobi in *Funeral of the Minstrel* are imagined. Parts of Esiaba's words in the dialogue in this play were actual words by the late writer taken from emails he wrote to Nnorom Azuonye, and some are taken from his published works. There are echoes of Irobi's *Nwokedi* in parts of this play and if any of the actors that played roles in that play interpret themselves into characters in *Funeral of the Minstrel*, that is all it is, an interpretation.

Preface
Esiaba Irobi, the Intellectual Terrorist

Funeral of The Minstrel was written at a time of great grief in my life. My teacher, mentor and friend, Dr Esiaba Irobi had just died in Berlin at the age of 49. The physical vehicle he used for his latest incarnation was still in storage in that German city and I found myself in London imagining what kind of funeral he might receive. This short play is that imagined scenario.

As a preface to this play, I have chosen to use *'Esiaba Irobi, the Intellectual Terrorist'* – a tributary article I wrote in 2010 which was published in Next newspaper. I believe that this article captures my respect for Esiaba Irobi, his work and his legacy.

'The Intellectual Terrorist' according to Esiaba, was the title of a novel he was writing. I don't know if he ever completed the book and if the world will ever see it. I chose to refer to Esiaba himself as the Intellectual Terrorist because of the several powerful and often violent plays he terrorized us with in his lifetime.

Health Warning: Some people may find aspects of the dialogue in this play a little vulgar or even rude. I have deliberately chosen not to disinfect Esiaba Irobi's mouth and the words that came out of it. I also suspect already that some people may judge my decision to publish such vulgar or rude words, being a preacher and all. I have done so because I am not one of those preachers who stand in front of their congregations and say things like; "I don't allow MTV in my house. I cannot let demons into my sitting room". I am a possibility preacher. I love my God and I share His word in sincerity, in freedom and in spirit. It is my prayer that all who hear the word of God will allow it to better their lives and possibly improve somebody else's life too.

The Intellectual Terrorist.

I don't really feel qualified to write about Esiaba Irobi. I have not met anyone quite qualified enough to write about Esiaba Irobi, the Minstrel. He represented something different to everyone he met. To many, he was the consummate artist and academic. To others he was a benchmark for hardwork and diligence. There were some who saw him as a spirit of anarchy. He was also a rude man who wrote many sexually-explicit poems with insane titles, my favourite being 'A Short History of my Penis.' I will attempt to write about the Esiaba Irobi I know. A good man. A laughter factory. A prophetic writer. A man who started out as my teacher, then became my friend, and ended up as my brother.

When I heard that Esiaba passed away. The news came via several text and voice messages on my phone, I stopped functioning. Literally stopped functioning. Everyone, all at once asked if I could confirm his death. Friends like Molara Wood and Toyin Adepoju among others wanted to be sure before calling the news by its name. I promised to find out from Esiaba's wife, Uloaku.

The phone call to Berlin was the most frightening call I have ever made, and in the spirit of the Minstrel, I was optimistic that Uloaku would chuckle and tell me there has been a big mistake. I was hoping it would be one of those celebrity deaths. A hoax. It turned out to be wishful thinking. Esiaba was gone. At first I was very strong. I even tapped into my strong belief in reincarnation and shrugged, "Well, Esiaba, it has been a tough journey for you. Go on, sir, reset your life and start over." Then I added, as we Ndi Igbo say when a person is going to our ancestors, "Esiaba, son of Irobi, your world, seven worlds, you will live your earthly life again. In your next life, you will not fall ill in mid-life. You will marry young, and raise your family in joy and good health. Go in peace, my brother."

It was really going well until I told my wife that Esiaba had died. Amaka had also grown close to Esiaba. Whenever he called our home, Amaka and Esiaba would laugh together on the phone as he performed poetry and songs for her down the line on international phone calls. My wife broke down on me and cried. That's when they gushed;

my first tears for Esiaba. Yes, I am a poet too and I am not afraid to have a good cry if it will stop my chest from exploding.

Nsukka

Esiaba Irobi was my lecturer in the Department of Dramatic Arts, University of Nigeria, Nsukka from between 1987 and 1989 when he left for the United Kingdom. He was more than a lecturer to me, he was an inspiration. Every course he taught me; Theatre History, Improvisation, Basic Acting Skills, and Introduction to Playwriting, opened my mind to the possibilities of the theatre.

Esiaba was not just a theorist, he showed us how to do what he taught. His performances were mesmerising. His energy was overwhelming. As an actor, he transformed even the lamest word in a play into a living entity inhabited by a spirit of dance. I had the privilege of understudying Esiaba as Elesi in Wole Soyinka's *Death and The King's Horseman*, a role he carried with commensurate pomp and passion. Under the out-of-this-world direction of Eni-Jones Umuko, Esiaba connected, raised and sustained the ritual impetus of that play, helped along with the magnificence of Nwugo Uzoigwe's Iyaloja. The air in the Arts Theatre at Nsukka was so taut through the performances that it could have strangled people.

The Plays

As a playwright, Esiaba wrote some of the angriest, action-packed, issue plays that packed theatres full every night. *Nwokedi, The Fronded Circle,* and *Hangmen Also Die* changed the theatre tradition at Nsukka forever. Those of us who dared pick up our pens to write plays were under the heavy influence of Esiaba Irobi. My own play, *'Rage of the Restless'* (yet unpublished) was essentially a clone of Esiaba's style and energy. I had small parts in *Nwokedi* as a Politician and member of the Ekumeku, but in *Hangmen Also Die*, I played the role of Chief Isokipiri Erekosima who embezzled three million Naira compensation money meant for the ordinary citizens of Izon State for the destruction of their livelihoods by oil spillage. Erekosima spent half a million of that money on his coronation alone, as the Amatemeso of Izon State, and some on paying for expensive lifestyles and education for his children abroad – because the standards of education in Nigeria had fallen. Chief Isokipiri Erekosima met his ancestors when The Suicide Squad, a band of unemployed graduates-turned-criminals kidnapped, tried, condemned and hanged him from a tree. *Hangmen Also Die* was produced in 1989, directed by Esiaba Irobi himself. Even back then, Esiaba foresaw the current crisis that has ravaged Nigeria's Niger Delta region. He was a prophet.

In 2003, I interviewed Esiaba and to the question 'Who is Esiaba Irobi?' he had replied; "He is from the Republic of Biafra and has lived all his life in exile in Nigeria, the United Kingdom and the USA. Everything he wrote in *Hangmen Also Die* has come to pass, including the hanging of the boys, the killing of the chiefs, the execution of Ken Saro-Wiwa in a prison in Port Harcourt. The recent revolt by riverain women against foreign oil companies in Nigeria reminds us strongly of Tamara in the play and also resonates with the reason for the iconoclastic philosophy of The Suicide Squad." He continued; "*Hangmen Also Die* is the most prophetic of all of Esiaba's works. It is a picture of the future. Our future as a country: Area Boys. Bakassi. Armed Robbery. Anarchy! The worst is yet to come. Nigeria will break apart like a loaf of bread in water, it will capsize like a leaking canoe on the River Niger!"

The Poetry

I first encountered the power of Esiaba's poetry at the Anthill, Nsukka, run back in the day by Gbubemi Amas, Big George and co. He would sing his words and on occasions break into powerful choruses and dance. He would break sweat performing a poem, and would ensure the poem was etched on the minds of members of the audience.

Following the publication of his seminal poetry collection; *Why I Don't Like Philip Larkin*, it was my honour to host him in London on April 1, 2006. Other poets that read on the same night were Toni Kan, Obemata, and Molara Wood. Their readings were punctuated with mine. It was all very good, but when Esiaba, the masquerade of the night stepped up to the stage, he turned the night on its head, with songs, with calls and responses, and with his lyrical pieces rendered with penetrating, seering power and conviction.

Esiaba wrote about some characters in his plays as people who used words "like a loaded pistol", but it was he, The Minstrel, a powerful wordsmith, who used words like a loaded pistol. Mixed and shaken, his words produced the effect of an atom bomb powerful enough to eradicate Nigeria's terminal diseases who populate the country's past, ruling and aspiring leadership.

Although Esiaba Irobi until his dying day felt convinced he was nothing but a Biafran man who only lived in exile in Nigeria, before continuing his exile in the United Kingdom, United States and Germany, where he was to go into transition, he never believed Nigeria as a country could survive, yet in my interview with him, he cared enough to prescribe a perfect solution to Nigeria's problems, saying: "What is needed are methodical and strategic insurrections.

Insurrections aimed at change. Permanent change. What the Irgun Stern gang did in Israel to the British. What the Mau Mau did in Kenya. Kamikaze pilots. Suicide Bombers. Coups. Against Nigerian leaders. What Nzeogwu did. What Sankara did. What Jerry Rawlings did. For example, Obasanjo and all the ministers and senators and local government chairmen and cheerwomen should be shaved upstairs and downstairs and put into a leaking boat and pushed into the Atlantic Ocean. Or members of the top military brass should be invited to meal/feast and fed from a pot laced with generous quantities of cyanide." He continued, "All the while, the younger generation should have alternative ethical and moral and progressive and visionary leadership – nobody should be above 40 years of age – to take over and save that country from extinction. As a matter of truth, I don't think that Nigeria as an entity will or can ever survive. It will at some point disintegrate like all good shit in a toilet bowl. That country has never worked. I don't think it will ever work."

Celebrating Esiaba
In 2009, Esiaba got married to the lovely Uloaku, who joined him in America in the summer. They moved together to Berlin where Esiaba took up position as a Distinguished Research Fellow, Freie University, Berlin, Germany 2009-2010 in the prestigious "Interweaving Performance Cultures"

programme at the University's International Research Centre.

The painful thing about Esiaba's life is that he was a man who had a habit of being happy always, no matter his situation. He worked very hard at his craft, and tried as much as he could to enjoy his life. Every time I was on the phone with Esiaba, or sat across the table for a bite or a drink, he had no idea how to be in somebody's company and not have a fun story to tell, a poem to read, a song to sing or a political or philosophical idea to banter over. I was quite aware that he was very well-respected in literary and academic circles, and had won some awards here and there, but it always surprised me that somehow, Esiaba had never really been publicly celebrated for all his achievements and vision. Therefore in 2009, I asked myself; should we wait for Esiaba to win at least one of the two Nobel Prizes for Literature he used to tell us he would win, before we celebrate him? Or should we celebrate him anyway? I chose the latter, and in the planning of the first Sentinel Literature Festival 1st – 4th of December 2009, we set aside December 4th as 'Esiaba Irobi Day.' The plan was simple: on that day, admirers of Esiaba Irobi and some of his former students would read their favourite Esiaba poems. Then there would be a musical interval, and then Esiaba himself would incinerate the place with a 60-minute performance.

I have never seen anyone as excited about an event as Esiaba was about the Esiaba Irobi Day at our festival. I am sure he won't mind my sharing some of his thoughts for the evening; "My sisters who live in London and my beautiful and lovely wife will cook/provide the food... I suggest very strongly that you change the picture of mine you have chosen. I will send another more exciting photograph which you can use to create a one-page advert in colour. You can then send it as an attachment – INDIVIDUALLY – to everybody who is interested in poetry in the UK...We can also target some Ngwa people who are not literary sensibilities but who will be coming for the food and the wine and the photograph-taking and to see their rambunctious brother performing in London with a band called The Republic of Biafra!...A lot of Igbo people – if you can find a listserv containing their names will also want to come...I also suggest that you push the event through Toyin Adepoju's Facebook. And the Wole Soyinka Society...Jackie Mackay knows a lot of people in the literary milieu of London. You should try and befriend her. She can help to swell the AUDIENCE on December 4, 2009. We should also think of special invitations to people like Peter Badejo, Osy Okagbue, Yvonne Brewster, Nigerian actors/ theatre directors, etc. The idea of Special Invitations and a kind of DISTINGUISHED high table and brief speeches about the poet will swell these people's heads and make them come as well as bring other people...I am planning to have food – Igbo cuisine on December 4. In addition, we can also have some wine, bread, cheese and charge a sensible gate fee for this huge event. I am planning to put on a really powerful show complete with my band: The Republic of Biafra. My son, Nnamdi, will play his saxophone in the band."

Published and forthcoming work

Esiaba also copied an e-mail he wrote to Jacqueline Mackay to me, and there, I thought we were about to celebrate Esiaba, only for me to learn he was dedicating the show to Ms Mackay. In this e-mail, he wrote, "I will not be "reading" but actually "performing" in the African oral tradition with my band: "The Republic of Biafra" excerpts from the following published and forthcoming collections: *Frozen Music* (1985), *Handgrenades* (1986), *Inflorescence* (1987), *Tenants of the Desert* (1988), *What is Tender about Ted Hughes?*(1989), *Is This a God I Smash?* (1990), *Tell Me I am Lying!*(1991), *The Kingdom of the Mad* (1997), *Why I Don't Like Philip Larkin* (2004), *A Calendar of Love* (forthcoming), *A Short History of my Penis* (forthcoming), *ZEZE and other LOVE poems* (forthcoming), *The Tree that Weeps* (forthcoming) ...It will be a great day and I will make it clear to everybody – before I begin my performance – that this event is specially staged for a great woman who has a lot of love for everything African including our literature, arts, cuisine, and young men with dysfunctional penises!"

He had it all planned in his head, but due to some unforeseen problems with his travel documents, he could not attend the festival and we had to cancel day 4. Esiaba Irobi day never happened and I hated to, but I refunded ticket fees.

In March 2010, I was delighted when Esiaba wrote me a heart-warming e-mail in which he said his health was on the mend, and he and his wife now had 5-year multiple visas in and out of Britain. Then the masterstroke: he informed me that his wedding had been fixed for the middle of June and that he would very much like me to organize a poetry event to serve as his bachelor's eve party. Like the festival show, Esiaba had big plans for his wedding poetry event, and after our last exchange on Wednesday the 28th of April, I started making plans to realise his big show in London, only this time, he did not just pull out due to visa problems, he actually did a Michael Jackson on me. Five days after our last e-mail exchange, Esiaba Irobi, the Minstrel passed away in Berlin.

Sentinel Poetry Movement
Whatever perceptions people now have of Sentinel Poetry Movement, it is a part of what has defined my life since 2002, and one thing I have

said at every opportunity I've got is that Esiaba Irobi was the one that suggested that I grow the idea from the small exercise on my website. I am happy that in his lifetime, Sentinel Poetry Movement published Esiaba's own poetry, and essays, as well as essays by others such as Pius Adesanmi and Afam Akeh on Irobi's works. I am also proud that although the big event never happened, there was that evening in 2006 when he sang and danced as part of a Sentinel Live event.

Eulogies

On hearing of his death, many have said wonderful things about Esiaba Irobi. The poet, Remi Raji describes him as "one of the finest but rarely sung writers." The truth is that we all wait for the West to adopt and celebrate our best. Esiaba was never going to be a darling of the western world. Our people are singing him now that he is dead. I however deeply appreciate some comments on my Facebook page from people I knew were genuine friends of the Minstrel; Dr Osita Okagbue writes, "With Esiaba some laughter has left; a joy for life and people has gone! I'll miss your laughter, our friend, colleague, and my academic nephew." Gbubemi Amas says, "This is very sad news for anyone who loves life." And among other tributes, Abdul Mahmud who writes as Obemata remembers him this way; "Esiaba was such an engaging poet;

memories of his performance at the maiden Sentinel Poetry Live years ago in London are as abiding as the fraternal love and respect he showed to some of us who interacted with him that night." That was Esiaba Irobi, a respecter of kindred spirits. A lover of life.

I am as devastated by Esiaba Irobi's passing as many of my colleagues and Esiaba's students are, but nothing we feel today can compare with what Uloaku, his wife of less than one year must feel, or what his Saxophone-playing son, Nnamdi, must feel. I also hope that Uloaku is well in the know about his unpublished works, and will work tirelessly to make sure they see the light of day. These include such books as *'How to make love to a Negro all Night and Survive it,' 'A White Man's Guide to Black Woman,' 'Theorizing African Cinema: Ontology, Teleology, Semiology and Narratology'* (Routledge, London), *'Before They Danced in Chains: African Metalanguages in African American Performance Aesthetics'* and his novel, too long in the making; *'The Intellectual Terrorist.'*

Nnorom Azuonye

funeral of the minstrel

The People

New Ekumeku (A group of 20 or more ex-students of Esiaba Irobi)

Maduka

Dike

Aloma

(Maduka, Dike and Aloma are Esiaba's ex-students, members of the New Ekumeku)

Earthquake (Esiaba's ex-student who predeceased him.)

Esiaba Irobi

Dede Okoronkwo (An Ngwa elder)

Onyebuchi (Leader of Esiaba's Age Grade)

Ezidiegwu (Age Grade member)

Chiehika (Age Grade member)

Esiaba's Age Grade members

The Action Sequence

The scenes in this play blend into each other. There are no breaks and no set changes. The stage is pitch black. Out of the darkness the sound of stamping feet and angry voices rise. Lights rise to reveal a casket draped with the flag of the Republic of Biafra up stage centre. There is a framed photograph of Esiaba Irobi leaning on the casket. Also on stage are members of Esiaba's Age Grade; about 10 to 15 men (depending on staging budget), within the age range of 40 to 50 years. Their feet stamping and chanting rise to a fever pitch. EZIDIEGWU stands aside to a corner of the stage and does not join the chanting or the stamping of feet. ONYEBUCHI leads and the rest respond as they go around the casket several times. They finally form a horseshoe downstage so that the casket is behind them and the lights dim on it.

Obu ngiri?
> Iwe.
Obu ngiri?
> Iwe.
Ajurum unu, obu ngiri?
> Iwe.
Ngiri?
> Iwe, iwe njuru anyi obi, iwe.
Obu ngiri ndi iwe anyi?
> Onwu.
Ngiri?
> Onwu. Onwu Esiaba, Onwu.

What is the matter?
    Anger.
What is the matter?
    Anger.
I ask you, what is the matter?
    Anger.
What?
    Anger. Our hearts are full of anger.
What is making us angry?
    Death.
What?
    Death. Esiaba's death. Death.

ONYEBUCHI: Stop. Stop. Quiet, my brothers. Quiet. You have spoken an abomination. Spit it away! You charge like angry lions. You say you are angry. Angry because of Esiaba's death. Death? What death? What death do you speak of? Spit! Spit away my brothers. Esiaba son of Irobi is not dead. He is not. I reject it in the name of Jesus. No. He is not dead.

EZIDIEGWU: Onyebuchi, big bros, all day you have been asking us; 'Why are you angry? Why are you angry?' My brother Onyebuchi, a man with scrotal elephantitis sits with the side of his buttocks. He sits with the side of his buttocks because he cannot deny the monstrosity between his legs. Try sitting with a tuber of yam between your legs. Why then do you pretend you don't know why our hearts and our spirits are broken? Do you honestly not know the reason our eyes bleed? When have you ever seen the toad running in the middle of the afternoon for no reason?

CHIEHIKA: Ezidiegwu, Ezidiegwu, please, please, let me stop you right there. Onyebuchi is not pretending. He knows the truth. Being who and what he is, Onyebuchi cannot believe this horrible story. He must not. If a grown man begins to weep at a funeral like a woman or a child, what then should the women and children do?

EZIDIEGWU: Why not, Chiehika? Why can't a grown man weep at a funeral? You people are unbelievable. In this day and age, you still behave like cave creatures. A man must never cry? Hear this, you savage cave man, a man's worth cannot be diminished by the tears he sheds in public, but by the evil he sees and pretends not to see. As our people say, when such a man dies, he begins to rot from eyes. Savages! Brutes! This is why I treat villagers with contempt.

CHIEHIKA: Are you not a villager yourself? Goat that treats animals with contempt! Just because you live in Aba, which is still Ngwaland, you think you are not a villager. You are worse than villagers because living in that slum in Aba, you cannot claim to be a township boy, and in your head you think you have left the village. A bat, that's what you are.

EZIDIEGWU: Don't insult me, Chiehika, don't insult me, or I swear on my father's life, this Ngwaland will drink your blood today.

CHIEHIKA: You swear on the life of somebody who has already died? You are not only ignorant, you are also bloodthirsty.

EZIDIEGWU: The oil is already spilt. We could stand here and threaten one another, or we could fetch mops and start cleaning. Can pregnancy be hidden from the eyes of the world by covering it with the palms of hands?

CHIEHIKA: You are the only one who has threatened somebody today, Ezidiegwu. You are not a child, my brother. This is our culture. He who bears the news that must not be called by its name, must roll his tongue inside his mouth, and whisper the news out from the corner of that mouth.

EZIDIEGWU: What is true is true. Esiaba has died. He walked the world to darkness in Berlin. That is the truth. Full stop.

CHIEHIKA: Ezidiegwu!

EZIDIEGWU: Yes?

CHIEHIKA: Roll your tongue inside your mouth...

EZIDIEGWU: Nonsense! Esiaba Irobi is dead. Bring out the masquerades to send him forth with the greatest show Ngwaland has ever seen.

ONYEBUCHI: Liar! Liar! Come with me. All of you, come, come with me. Let's go and look for him. Esiaba has been travelling for a long time. The traveller spat on the ground before he set off. We must find him, and we must urge him to come home before the saliva dries and causes his navel to begin to rot.

EZIDIEGWU: You know what? You may carry on with your primitive culture. Just count me out. Count me out. I am a realist. Full stop. When will our people stop this practice of twisting the neck of truth? An old man dies, a message is sent to his son living abroad; "come home quickly, papa is very sick and wants to see you desperately." Why can't we just say things as they are? So, please spare me this cultural thing and stop talking as if Esiaba is still alive. What we must do now is begin the process of giving his body a befitting burial.

ONYEBUCHI: He is alive. Ezidiegwu, I think you have gone mad. You must stop smoking that evil weed you smoke in Ariaria market.

EZIDIEGWU: You are the mad one! Twenty-first century Thomas. I tell you, Esiaba's body will fall on your head and knock it down into your chest and you will still say he is alive. Mad man. Thomas!

ONYEBUCHI: *(Stares at Ezidiegwu with disdain, and chooses to ignore him)* We must now send the silent message of our forefathers to Esiaba. He will hear the call and start coming home.

CHIEHIKA: Onyebuchi, I am not on Ezidiegwu's side, you know that. But what if he is…what if he really is, you know…

EZIDIEGWU: Dead? Call it by its name, coward.

ONYEBUCHI: If Esiaba is dead, he will hear the music of our forefathers rising from the village square. He will hear the broken beats of our hearts. Yes, he will hear us; a choir of grown men weeping like women and children. Then he shall return this very day, to bid farewell to the land of Ngwa, to feed her earth. But he is not…

There is distant drumming coming from the rear of the auditorium. ONYEBUCHI pauses and stares blankly into the dark for a heartbeat. Then continues…

ONYEBUCHI: Did I just hear the drums of lamentation from the other side of life? Did I hear them or do my ears deceive me? Has our pridebearer traded his colourful clothes for the dull and the drab? Show me the songmaster who can make a song with his voice trapped in a box.

The drumbeats rise again and rise into a deafening frenzy. All on stage freeze and stare into the distance beyond the audience. The drumming suddenly stops. Onyebuchi, Chiehika and Ezidiegwu thaw and come together and begin to whisper to each other. Suddenly they scatter to different part of the stage snapping their fingers around their heads.

ONYEBUCHI: *(finally speaks but does not look at the others. He is looking up to the sky as if he is addressing God.)* If it is true. Ah! If it is true that Esiaba Irobi is dead, I shall urinate hot urine into the thirsty gullet of this land, so that the meat of Esiaba's body shall bear witness against it. This land that should fight the accuser on our behalf, this land that must say to that spirit Esiaba himself once described as a vandal, 'I am not ready to receive Esiaba's body, he has many years to live, he still has a lot more to say, he still has not won his Nobel Prize. No, he still has not won his two Nobel Prizes for literature.' He promised to win the Nobel Prize for Literature twice. *(Weeping)* Oh, if the spirit of this land did not fight to keep breath in Esiaba's lungs, today, I Onyebuchi, first son of Ahamba, shall urinate hot urine into her gullet. *(Turns to Chiehika, Ezidiegwu and the other members of Esiaba's Age Grade)* Let's go.

CHIEHIKA *(Leads the new chant)*

Ngwa anyi nje.

　　　Anyi nje l'olee?

Anyi nje icho Esiaba nwa Irobi,

　　　ngwa anyi nje.

Let us go

　　　Where are we going to?

We are going to look for Esiaba son of Irobi,

　　　Let us go.

33

*They chant and stamp their feet hard on the ground
and leave the stage. Lights rise upstage to reveal
DEDE OKORONKWO with his head bent, and his
two hands on the casket. He is shaking his head from
side to side as the angry voices of Esiaba's age grade
fade out. He disengages from the casket and addresses
Esiaba, walking around the casket, gesticulating. In the
background a dirge simmers. The director or
production company may choose a dirge of their own
liking, or use this one:*

Udu m etiwala o tiwala
Ezigbo udum etiwala, o tiwala
o tiwara n'ike.
Agbagbuola ha ugo
Agbagbuola ha ugo bere n'oji
Agbagbuola ha ugo
Udu m etiwala o tiwala
Ezigbo udu m etiwala
O tiwara n'ike.

*My earthen pot is broken
My precious earthen pot is broken
It is broken by force
They have shot dead the eagle
They have shot dead the eagle on iroko
They have shot dead the eagle
My earthen pot is broken
My precious earthen pot is broken
It is broken by force*

DEDE OKORONKWO: Esiaba. Esiaba nwa Irobi, you have done it all wrong. I search the face of the sky for answers. The only thing I see is that you were not ready. You were not ready! You were ambushed by a master trickster and he beat you.

(The dirge rises and then fades out)

Only last month, I received a copy of your poetry book; *Why I Don't Like Philip Larkin*, and you had kindly made a handwritten note to me on the first page; 'Dee Okoronkwo, read *A Ceramic Life*. Just remove Chukwudi Eboh's name and slot in your wife's name. It may not comfort you. How can words comfort you, when your soulmate has died?'

(The dirge rises, lingers for a little while and then fades out)

Oh, Esiaba, how I wish I had the power to send a telegram to that cursed vandal. If I could, my telegram would read, 'you have devoured my friend, I shall cut you down like the evil tree you are, burn you to cinders and scatter your ashes into the four winds and your name shall be deleted permanently from our consciousness.' That's what my telegram will read.

He wipes his eyes. The dirge rises and is sustained for about one minute, then simmers.

Or were you sending a message to me? Were you telling me you were to join my dear Urediya? Esii, I read what you wrote for your friend:

35

"Chukwudi Eboh, on the day you died,
Death sent me a telegram. In it the vandal wrote:
"I have devoured your friend, I now wait for you."

Esii, that vandal sees no point in writing telegrams anymore; telegrams can be crumpled between angry fingers. They can be thrown with contempt into trash cans.

The dirge rises and is sustained for about one minute, then simmers.

He has learnt to box and kick, bite and claw. The hooligan thrives on crimson juices, like volcanic vomit oozing from every wound on the battered body of earth. The vandal swaggers, like all undisputed despots do, from continent to continent he snatches breaths and spits dirty spit on glowering embers. Oh, nature! Why are you not fair? Esiaba Irobi is half my age, how I wish I could take his place, and he be here, full of life, audacious, with his special way with words, every word a grenade exploding every conscience to life; to what is right. It should be Esiaba speaking at my funeral, as I, the old grist, get flushed away from the mill of life.

The dirge rises and is sustained for about one minute, then simmers.

He breaks legs that dance to the music of gods. At his mischievous best he would punch out a poet, knee him in the chest and stuff his mouth with his beddings, beddings unlaundered in a million years. *(Pauses)* Oh, how I wish I could give him a slap across his smirking ugly face. A dirty slap. Then banish him to unquenchable fires of hell…

He is interrupted by the singing of an energetic Ekpe song and suddenly a group of about twenty men and women enter. The men all have glistening machetes thrusting in front of them as they dance unto the stage towards Dede Okoronkwo.

DEDE OKORONKWO: *(Shouting over their song)* Who are you people? Who are you people? Where have you come from?

They pull him further down the stage and continue to dance around him, waving their machetes at him. Finally they stop and form a horseshoe between him and the casket.

DEDE OKORONKWO: Who are you people?

MADUKA: We are the New Ekumeku.

DEDE OKORONKWO: There is no such thing as New Ekumeku.

MADUKA: There is now. We were created by Esiaba Irobi, the Minstrel, we are -

ALOMA: Whirlwind! That's what we are. We are the new whirlwind.

DIKE: *(Waving a machete at Dede Okoronkwo.)* And in our powerful cyclical arms we carry rotten news away and cast it into the Atlantic Ocean.

MADUKA: We are here to carry your rotten news away.

DEDE OKORONKWO: And are you able to make the dead live?

ALOMA: The dead? Did you say 'the dead'? *(Looking around)* Has anybody died?

DEDE OKORONKWO: My children, I am sorry, you have gatecrashed a funeral. The funeral of the Minstrel, Esiaba Irobi. Did you say he created you?

Together, the members of the New Ekumeku snap their fingers around their heads.

NEW EKUMEKU: Tufia kwa! Tufia! Esiaba Irobi is not dead.

MADUKA: Esiaba Irobi and dead are words that do not belong in one sentence.

DEDE OKORONKWO: It is not fair, my children, but everybody dies. Some die young. Some die old. Esiaba has died young.

DIKE: *(Takes steps towards Dede Okoronkwo, pointing his machete at him).* Take back your words old man or I will decapitate you and feed your head to the beasts of the jungle. The body that houses the mouth that speaks abomination shall belong to termites. The termites, old man, do you hear me? Take back your words.

DEDE OKORONKWO: *(Calmly)* My son, put down the machete before you hurt somebody.

DIKE: *(Barking)* Take back your words.

ALOMA: Dike, put down your machete now. Are you mad? Can't you see he is a titled man? A respected member of Esiaba's community? Did Esiaba not teach you anything?

DIKE: Did Esiaba not teach me anything? For twenty-two years, I have been eating, drinking, breathing in and living Esiaba Irobi's words. Remember, the great Nwokedi put a machete on the neck of his own father. Did Esiaba not teach me anything? Was Nwokedi senior not a titled man?

ALOMA: And what has that got to do with this madness you display today? Have you not read the question Esiaba asked Salman Rushdie in his poem Sisyphus; "…is nothing really sacred? / Do people not need a faith? A god, even if it is made of iron / they can worship?" We are Igbo people. We may not have kings but we respect age, and we respect men and women who have earned their titles. It is sacrilege to threaten a titled man in Igbo land with a machete. This is not what Esiaba wants from us.

DIKE: I cannot threaten a titled man even when his words are abominable?

MADUKA: Yes, even when his words are abominable. I agree with Aloma. Put down your machete.

DEDE OKORONKWO: My son, what is your name?

DIKE: *(Rising to his toes and raising the machete high into the air)* I am Nwokedi.

NEW EKUMEKU: Nwokedi?

DIKE: Yes. Nwokedi. There is magic in my name.

ALOMA: Is your name not Dike?

DIKE: In another life, yes, but in this life I live at the moment. I am Nwokedi, a child of the Minstrel.

(New Ekumeku suddenly begin to shuffle-dance, their machetes in front of them as they sing, 'Nwokedi o, onye ogburu o laa, onyike' They return to their positions.)

DIKE: Yes, I am Nwokedi. I am the spirit of revolution in this land. I am the blade that will shave corruption off the head of this land. I am that blade that will shave the corrupt leaders of our land upstairs and downstairs before we push them into the Atlantic Ocean in a leaking canoe, as Esiaba Irobi instructed. Esiaba Irobi is the great artificer that created me, he cannot die. He is indestructible. Can a world outlive the god that created it?

DEDE OKORONKWO: Nwokedi? Nwokedi! I remember you now. You are a character in one of Esiaba's plays. You are a fictional character in a play.

DIKE: *(Moves away angrily and faces the audience)* I am not a fictional character in a play. I am Nwokedi. I am as real as the sun and the stars. I am The Rising Sun, the immortal emblem of the Republic of Biafra. I am that which exists that cowards don't want to acknowledge. *(Pointing to Maduka)* This man is Sir Walter Raleigh, and this woman, *(pointing to Aloma)* is my dear mother, Mama Nwokedi.

MADUKA: In the play, Dike. We are not acting a play now. What has come over you?

ALOMA: He is possessed. Possessed by the spirit of Nwokedi.

DIKE: I am not possessed. I am Dike. I know who I am. *(Pauses)* O.K. I am a little possessed. I must admit. Today, I am Nwokedi. If Esiaba is really sleeping in that box *(points at the casket)*, with this machete I shall cut the box open and wake him up.

ALOMA: Wake him up? How are we going to wake up somebody who is not sleeping? That is not what we came here to do.

MADUKA: We came here to carry the bad news away. We came here to tell the people of Ngwa, Esiaba's family, Esiaba's friends, Esiaba's fans, that they must not look for Esiaba in a wooden box, because he is not there. That's it. We did not come here to behead anybody. We did not come here to exercise the first power.

DIKE: The first power! What the hell is the first power?

MADUKA: The power to resurrect the dead.

ALOMA: Esiaba Irobi, the Minstrel, is dead. Long live Esiaba Irobi, the Minstrel. He lives! He lives in that form which cannot be hurt or killed. He has become song. Song in the hearts of men. Song in bookshelves. Song in the wind. The Minstrel has become song. I feel like shouting Halleluya! The Minstrel has become a song.

DIKE: I will wake him. He is only sleeping. *(Weeping)* I will wake him. I will wake him up. *(He breaks down, weeping uncontrollably. Maduka and Aloma move to him and begin to comfort him)*

At that moment, Esiaba is heard chanting and responding to himself, and stamping his foot on the floor as he enters from a door Down Stage Right...

ESIABA: *(His face is bright with a wide smile.)*
Nzogbu Nzogbu,
Enyimba, Enyi,
Nzogbu,
Enyimba Enyi.
(He stops and waves at the audience)
Ngwaland, Enyi Mba, asim unu, Nzogbu Nzogbu, Enyimba enyi.

Esiaba circles Dede Okoronkwo and the New Ekumeku. They stare at him in disbelief. Then he stretches out his hand to shake Dike's hand. As their hands touch, Dike leaps off the ground with a loud scream and falls unto the stage floor.

ESIABA: *(Laughing out uncontrollably)* Did I shock you? Dike of the universe, I am now electricity. Listen, now you have a Weapon of Corrupt Leaders Destruction – WCLD! Any time you feel frustrated enough, and angry enough by the betrayal of leaders of this country…did I say country? Forgive me, I meant cuntry. Just call my name, Esiaba Irobi, and I will be there to electrocute the pricks for you. Every single one of them beginning with that grotesque farm king that fucked Biafra. I will happily electrocute that ugly head of a diseased penis for you, as I will take pleasure in frying the homicidal gap-toothed genius standing like a plague in his designer axis of evil, his rod in his hand, masturbating, as he plots his next wickedness. I will electrocute them all. Just ask.

NEW EKUMEKU & DEDE OKORONKWO: Esiaba!

ESIABA: As you can see, a box cannot hold me. What that lifeless form in the box is doing, can we call it sleep? Look, people are watching you, my friends, as you do what you do to honour me.

43

Some will say you are a bunch of over-emotional imbeciles. Some will say grief has made you mad. But it is really very atavistic, is it not? Go back and subject our history to forensic investigation, it is full of tales of great warriors, artists and leaders, real leaders, not the kind of cunts and baboons you see in Aso Rock these days, they were sent off with pomp, wit and anger, even savagery! Look, many coffins of great men dance without a sway upon the skulls of young men's heads brought to the funerals by angry mourners, is this not true? I am talking about heads harvested with shimmering scimitars. If you place my coffin on the skulls of twelve young men to honour me as a literary king, people will object and call you savages and murderers, but when one of those traditional rulers goes to sleep with his equally useless ancestors, his coffin will rest on the heads of twenty men and they call it culture. That is your bloody country, is it not? Listen, don't get me wrong, I am very happy today because you are angry that I am no longer with you the way I used to be. I am happy because you have shining machetes glinting under the fiery eyes of Ngwa sun today. I am even happier because you have not used the machetes on anyone. That would be to miss the point in everything I have taught you.

MADUKA: Esiaba, but how you come fuck up like this now? Man, you really fuck up.

ALOMA: Is it his fault that he died? It is not his fault.

DIKE: Shut up Aloma. How is it not his fault? He promised us that he would be eternal.

ESIABA: Thank you. I am eternal. Look, anyone who pays attention to his environment, like I did. Anyone who is not too busy sucking his own dick, like I never did. Anyone who sees the cancer eating the society to death, and raises a voice against it, like I did, he too will become eternal. (*Chuckles*) Especially if he brings a penetrating intelligence, like I did, to every argument. It is simple my friends. If your country is being ruled by arseholes, say it is ruled by arseholes. Don't say it in such a way that the arseholes will read it and not even know you are talking about them. I said this before, of course, in my poem; 'Kingdom of the Mad.' In that poem, I wrote:

> Join me Femi Osofisan,
> from your office in Ibadan.
> As I told you at Leeds,
> the Monsters of the deep are still
> feeding on my soul like the teeth
> of a thousand piranhas.
>
> Femi, I hope when I die, someone will
> stand at my graveside and recite with
> a tremulous voice, this epitaph:

We have gathered here today, in Aba
to mourn a stubborn poet called Esiaba,
who deeply believed that there comes
a time in every poet's career
when he or she must have the guts
to call a cunt a cunt
even if it is his own fucked-up cuntry.

NEW EKUMEKU & DEDE OKORONKWO:
(Together) We have gathered here today, in Aba,
to mourn a stubborn poet called Esiaba,
who deeply believed that there comes
a time in every poet's career
when he or she must have the guts
to call a cunt a cunt
even if it is his own fucked-up cuntry.

ESIABA: *(Breaks into a song and dance)* Onye adola
Esiaba aka n'utu, ma odi ndu, ma onwuru anwu,
onye adola Esiaba aka n'utu.

New Ekumeku members join Esiaba in singing the
song and dancing around the stage. Dede Okoronkwo
stands to one side, looking at them and shaking his
head in disbelief. They sing and dance for about two
minutes and then stop.

ALOMA: *(Weeping)* But you still had so much to
give, and so much to live for. This is not fair. It is
not fair at all.

ESIABA: Fair is a word that life does not understand. The reaper said to the custodian of breath, 'I am going for the Minstrel', and he reaped a nod of the oldest and wisest head. That was not fair. The collectors cut off the air supply to the vessel in that casket, *(pointing at the casket with contempt)* and I was angry. I was angry because I was at the happiest point in my life. I smiled through my weekly chemotherapy because I knew my other half, my prayer warrior, Uloaku, was with me. My God was also with me. *(Pauses)* You may wonder what Esiaba Irobi and God have to do with each other. That woman, that woman, Uloaku, showed me the power of prayer. Many times I even heard the voice of God. Trust me. He exists. *(Pauses)* Oh, Uloaku. *(Looks around the audience).* Where is Uloaku? Where is Uloaku? *(His voice breaks)* Uloaku is not here to bid me farewell? *(Solemnly)* Does anybody know why? *(He searches the faces of the audience and the New Ekumeku).* I wonder what primitive machination is going on. *(He falls silently and paces around the stage in silence, in deep thought.)* Anyway, it doesn't matter. God bless that woman. Only God knows what that young woman bore for me in the little time we spent together. I charge you my friends, my family, my fans, to be kind to her. *(Then he sees his muse, Georgina, among the mourners)* Oh there you are Georgie of the World! You always wanted me to come back to this country, did you not? In a thousand letters, a million phone calls, in countless dreams, you urged me to come back here. But as you can now see, Georgie, the Almighty God shares the same sense of humour as Zeus, and Amadioha. They have sent me back alright. You can see me, but you can't have me. You can't even spend time in the dead of the night to critique my new play; *The Dickheads of Ngwa Land*, the one I told you about, a whip against the backsides of all those shameless young men from our land who have made kidnapping of honest, hardworking citizens of this land a growth industry. It is a bloody shame. What kind of idiot makes a living from kidnapping another human being and claiming a ransom on his head? I am so ashamed to know that the Ngwa axis has become the kidnap capital of Nigeria. *(Looks straight at the audience)* What is wrong with you people? Georgie of the world, I promise you, I promise you, the woman I should have married, that I will possess another playwright to write it, and it will sting like alligator pepper. Even those idiots who are not the theatre-going types will eat and swallow *The Dickheads of Ngwa Land*, and the only things they will kidnap afterwards will be books, and they will imagine this country out of its rot and shit. I shall possess somebody.

(He sings):

'This world is not my home.
I am just passing through,
but I hope I have left my mark,

words to live forever...' *(stops singing suddenly)*

If you love me, don't just read the words I have written, perform them, always perform them, as you know, poetry is not only sonic, at its best it is performative. So, to read my words without action is like having sex wearing a condom, that you know, will never bear any fruit.

Don't let my work be just words.
Let them teach.
Let them change somebody.
Let them save somebody.
Even one person is enough.
Remember everything I said to you, Georgie.

He pauses to wipe tears from his eyes, turns to New Ekumeku

Where was I? What was I saying? Ah, yes, after a while I realized that I had only been taken away from a rickety jalopy fucked-up by cancer, and already screwed by diabetes before that. I was sent into this awesome space. Where I exist now, I feel no pain, I don't need food, I don't need drink, I don't even need sex, no need to come and go all night. Here, no man will ever again feel the shame on the occasions that his ogbunigwe fails to detonate and he worries that his woman will go away wondering whether he is a man or not. Here, none of those things matters. I now have access to all knowledge. I am just fine. Georgie of the world, tell Uloaku this, tell her I said "if God did not know you would all be alright, if God did not know that my son, Nnamdi would be alright, he would not have allowed them to take me."

Georgie of the world. Do you remember the poem I wrote for you, 'Homecoming,'? It is in my book, *Why I Don't Like Philip Larkin*. I wrote to you in that poem:

"GEORGIE OF THE WORLD,
I shall return to you at ebbtide
    When the crocodiles have left the shore
And the crabs of democracy have waddled back
    Into the swamp where they belong.
…
The cotyledon transplanted to a foreign land,
The minstrel who can only return at ebbtide. At ebbtide."

I have returned. My love. I have returned, but I don't belong to you anymore. I am now a song for everyone.

NEW EKEMEKU: But Esiaba, what about us, we are not alright, Esiaba. We are not alright at all.

ESIABA: You will be. Just look inside my books. Read between the lines in my plays and my poems. There are secret messages there for you.

Messages that will help you prepare for the war ahead…

Esiaba's Age Grade led by Onyebuchi enter still singing their 'Iwe' song. They suddenly stop as they see Esiaba.

ONYEBUCHI: Esiaba!

ESIABA: Onyebuchi. Why is your face like the face of a prostitute who has worked all night without pay?

ONYEBUCHI: Why is my face like what? Do you think this is a joking matter?

ESIABA: What is it that is not a joking matter?

ONYEBUCHI: Your death.

ESIABA: Man is spirit. Man never dies. Man can however fail to proceed with a particular body. This is what has happened. I am not dead, cheer up.

OBIEHIKA: Ezidiegwu, what did I tell you?

Just then Earthquake appears by a door up stage left. He is bathed in bright lights, and he stretches out his hands towards Esiaba.

EARTHQUAKE: Esiaba nwa Irobi –

ESIABA: Earthquake! Are you still in the great beyond? I would have thought by now you might have reincarnated.

EARTHQUAKE: I was about to be birthed afresh when the trumpet of honour sounded at the Diamond Theatre.

ESIABA: What is the Diamond Theatre?

EARTHQUAKE: The biggest playhouse you can ever imagine. All the worthy people of our art work there until it is time for them to return to earth to live their earthly lives again. I have been asked to usher you in. Especially at this time of great excitement.

ESIABA: Tell me who is there at the moment and why is this a great time of excitement?

EARTHQUAKE: If you are curious about Jazz Amankulor, he is waiting for you. In fact, he is directing your play *The Fronded Circle* there, and three of your students; Emmanuel Mogor, Livina Dimuna and Godfrey Okoro are in it.

ESIABA: What about Arthur Miller and Harold Pinter?

EARTHQUAKE: They are there too, waiting for you. Everyone who is anyone in the theatre that has bowed out of this world is waiting for you. Your reputation precedes you, Esiaba, you are at once a bad boy and a high priest of our art. Come, come, come, and take your place as a distinguished custodian of the creative cosmos.

ESIABA: That is good because I am sure there will be some of those Harvard and Princeton creative art residues there, the flotsam and jetsam of the theatre I can harass and upset. They are, as you might already know, the subject of one of the books I was working on titled *Harvard, Princeton and African Poetry*. It is based on an experience I had in Berlin in December 2009. These four bastards, two from Harvard and two from Princeton told me there is really no such thing as African poetry. I spent the next fifteen minutes teaching them something. I taught them to say, nsi nkita. *(Laughs)* When they had learnt to say nsi nkita very well, I asked them to say it whenever I raised my arm. *(Clears his throat)* So, Dike and Maduka, come here and be my Harvard and Princeton friends.

Dike and Maduka step forward and stand near Esiaba.

ESIABA: My Harvard friends are *(Raises arm)*

DIKE & MADUKA: Nsi nkita

ESIABA: My Princeton friends are *(raises arm)*

DIKE & MADUKA: Nsi nkita

ESIABA: The thing you know, the thing you call poetry is a big pile of *(raises arm)*

DIKE & MADUKA: Nsi nkita

ESIABA: Your history, the history of your land, your people are all *(raises arm)*

DIKE & MADUKA: Nsi nkita

ESIABA: The four of you standing here are *(raises arm)*

DIKE & MADUKA: Nsi nkita

ESIABA: Four Chimpanzees *(does not raise arm this time.)* It was hilarious. One of them asked, 'What was that? Did he just call us chimpanzees?' and I said, Yes, I did. The clown protested, 'Man, you are out of line.' That's when I asked them; do you know what nsi nkita really means? And one of them said, 'Did you not say 'erudite professors'?' Oh no, did I say that? I asked, it means 'dog shit.' You bloody piss heads, you insult everything you don't understand.

.

EARTHQUAKE: Nice story Esiaba, but we must go now.

ESIABA: I will go with you. This very day I shall turn the Diamond Theatre on its head. I will pierce many hearts with razor-sharp words. I will turn the anger of bitter spirits into laughter. I will shake up whatever stuffy traditions Shakespeare, Marlowe and Hubert Ogunde have set up. This very day, they will know that the most exciting, sexiest, and most engaging iconoclastic icon who traversed two centuries has arrived…

EARTHQUAKE: Esiaba nwa Irobi, leave it to history to analyse and eulogise you. Even now, the young men of your age grade are getting ready to commit your body to earth. Earth must return to earth for life to continue. *(Voice vibrating)* Come! Come! Come!

Esiaba begins to take tentative steps towards Earthquake. A dirge hummed by New Ekumeku and members of the Age Grade simmers in the background. Again, the director/producer may use a dirge of their choice, but this one will work nicely:

O lawala, O lawala
Laa n'udo
O lawala, O lawala
Laa n'udo
Nwanne anyi nwoke alawala

O lawala n'udo
Esiaba Irobi a lawala
O lawala n'udo

He is going home, he is going home
Go in peace
He is going home, he is going home
Go in peace
Our brother is going home
He is going home in peace
Esiaba Irobi is going home
He is going home in peace.

DEDE OKORONKWO: Ewoo. Esiaba!

ESIABA: *(Stops. Without looking at him.)* Dede.

DEDE OKORONKWO: Fare you well my son. I shall live out my days relieved because I have seen you, because I can see you are alright, because I can see you are not a broken spirit wallowing in self-pity, because you are not bitter.

ESIABA: Thank you, Dede.

DEDE OKORONKWO: Yet it shall not be good for that vandal.

ESIABA: Death's job is to kill; to destroy glittering and promising lives. To inflict pain. To cause grief. When he takes a person like me, the fool deludes himself that he will earn plaudits from the perverse high council of the disembodied. What he does not know is that anyone who has not buried his talents in the ground can never be bound by the end of earthly life. Think about such people as Aeschylus, Sophocles, Aristophanes. Shakespeare, Marlowe, Beckett, Okigbo, Nwoga, Miller, Pinter. Esiaba Irobi. We are really the meaning of the question: Death, where is your sting?

The dirge rises again as Esiaba gets closer to Earthquake.

EARTHQUAKE: The song that primes our path wanes, Esiaba, what is it that holds you back?

ESIABA: I am coming, Earthquake, I am coming. You have walked this walk before. You know it is not easy.

DEDE OKORONKWO: The patience of your usher grows thin, my son. Go on to greater glory and watch from there and see the mustard seeds you sowed grow into giant trees that will entertain, amuse and educate generations across centuries. Go, my son, explore creation's wonders as you have never seen them before. Go, go to glory.

Esiaba now stands next to Earthquake. The dirge simmers in the background.

DEDE OKORONKWO: Now we must prepare to commit that jalopy of yours to earth and feed the termites. As we feed them, we shall also curse them for devouring a jewel of a body. Even today, antkind will give praise to nature for the privilege of eating you. A million years from now, mankind will still be surprised, shocked, amused and instructed by your songs, your poetry, your plays and your essays. Goodbye Esiaba.

All turn towards Esiaba, with their backs to the audience. Esiaba and Earthquake are now in the bright light together.

ESIABA: Georgie of the world. Dike of the universe. Maduka. Aloma. Onyebuchi. Dede Okoronkwo, and all of you my students, my friends, my age grade, Ngwa people. Thank you for coming here today to send me forth to the other world. I know the one question you all want to ask: Do I have any regrets? Yes, I do. I regret that the sun did not rise again on the Republic of Biafra in my lifetime. Yet I am happy because I never for once stopped flying the flag of my nation, even while I lived in exile in Nigeria, and throughout my years of exile in Britain, and the United States of America. When the sun rises again, engage my living will to be celebrated as a

Biafran writer and performer. Don't let them get history wrong with me as they have with Christopher Okigbo. He died as a Biafran soldier, but he is celebrated as a Nigerian poet. I regret that I did not grow old with my lovely wife, Uloaku. I regret that I did not get to know my son better, and he did not get to know me better. It hurts me that my son Nnamdi shall spend the next few years hearing about what a great guy his father was. It hurts. I must however find a way to be with him always.

The dirge rises, New Ekumeku, the Age Grade, and Dede Okoronkwo raise their arms and begin to wave goodbye to Esiaba.

ESIABA: I must go now. One final thing. Earthquake, I know you are impatient, but I must say this to my fellow Biafrans, especially the Igbo people. For the record, I wrote this in an email to Nnorom Azuonye; "Let us continue to work together despite the incipient problems we have encountered. In fact it will give me a lot of joy if we can continue to work together and defy the Igbo jinx of not being able to support each other."

My final wish is that every one of you must look inward today, ask yourself who you are and what legacy you must bequeath to the world. Identify it. Deliver it. Be happy. That is an order. O.K. O.K.

Oh, one more thing, tell Nnorom Azuonye that he still needs to go ahead with the Esiaba Irobi Day he envisioned. I really like the sound of that. If he can pull it off and get all the literary types together under one roof to celebrate this rambunctious songmaster, that will be better than the Nobels I did not hang around long enough to claim. Remember me as I was in life – PURE JOY – Esiaba Irobi, the Minstrel.

(Raising his voice)

Who is the person in that lighting booth? Is that Okwudili Anagboso or Domba Asomba? Put out the goddamn house lights.

BLACKOUT.

www.ingramcontent.com/pod-product-compliance
Lightning Source LLC
Chambersburg PA
CBHW020607030426
42337CB00013B/1252